THE CHANGING

Chipping Morton

BOOK ONE

Julie Kennedy

SERIES
NUMBER
42

Robert Boyd
PUBLICATIONS

Published by
Robert Boyd Publications
260 Colwell Drive
Witney, Oxfordshire OX8 7LW

First published 2000

Copyright © Julie Kennedy and
Robert Boyd Publications

ISBN: 1 899536 46 9

Printed and bound in Great Britain at
The Alden Press, Oxford

OTHER TITLES IN THE *CHANGING FACES* SERIES

FORTHCOMING

Do you want to publish a book?

It is not as difficult as you might think. The publisher of this book provides a service to individuals and organisations, large and small.

Advice can be given on all facets of book production.

If you have a project you would like to discuss why not contact:

Robert Boyd
PRINTING & PUBLISHING SERVICES
260 Colwell Drive
Witney
Oxfordshire
OX8 7LW

Contents

Front cover photograph

Percy Sims (with camera) prepares to take a photograph.

Back cover photograph

A view from the High Street.

Acknowledgements

I would like to thank all those who have helped with this book including: Chipping Norton Historical Society; Oxfordshire County Council, Photographic Archives especially Dr. Malcolm Graham and Nuala La Vertue; Reed Information Service and Sheila Stewart for permission to quote from *Lifting the Latch*. Oxfordshire County Council hold an enormous number of photographs in the Frank Packer Collection.

The following have spent a long time sharing their memories with me as well as unearthing photographs: Julie Ashworth, John and Anna Betteridge, Elaine Boddington, Alan Brain, Stella and Laurie Burden, Don Davidson, Joan and Gilbert Giles, John Hannis, Maureen Hannis, Michael Hannis Eric Hood, Dick and Muriel Gibbs, John Grantham, Daphne Lay, Les Leach, Harry Pickett, Gay Scroggs, Lily Senear, Jim and Barbara Shepard, Ron Stares, Brenda and Cyril Smart, Mavis and Angus Stephen and Keith Vickers. I would also like to thank my husband Pete for his memories of life in Chipping Norton when he worked for the Borough Council and Ben, Erin, Rafe and Leo for their support. This book is dedicated to the memory of my mother in law, Joyce Kennedy, who is remembered with great affection by many in Chipping Norton.

Preface

Although the origins of Chipping Norton are lost in the mists of time, it is almost certain that some kind of community has inhabited this region since at least the first century AD. The early eleventh century saw the building of a castle which survived until the end of the middle ages, the foundations of which were situated near the site of the present church. By c 1450 Chipping Norton was established as a wool market. In 1606 Chipping Norton became a borough, this system lasting for over 350 years until the Local Government reorganisation in 1974.

Chipping Norton was once a self-sufficient town, its many shops supplying the outlying villages and goods being taken there by delivery men. Subject to the weather, Chipping Norton could be, and frequently was, cut off by heavy snow falls, especially in 1947 and 1963. Employment was to be found on farms, at Bliss' Tweed Mill, in Hitchman's brewery or Hubb's ironworks or on the railway, in addition to the commercial side. Today the railway is long gone, farms are no longer labour intensive and even the shops have less employees.

In the past few years the shops have been modernised, attracting shoppers from a wide area as well as tourists who visit the Cotswold area. Pubs, restaurants, a swimming pool and a theatre offer diverse recreational and social activities coupled with the societies that meet in the town. Many of the town's occupants work outside the area, but the increase in new housing attests to the popularity of Chipping Norton.

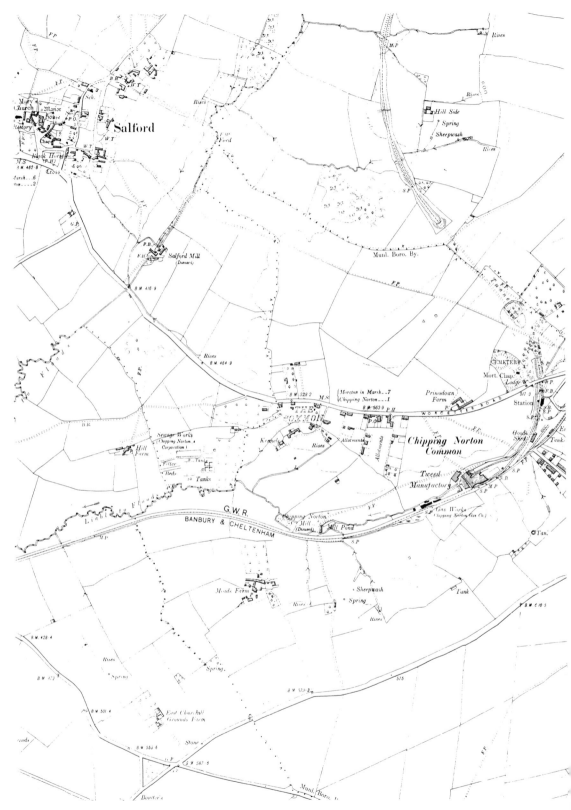

An Ordnance Survey map of 1922.

Introduction

Chipping Norton has been self-sufficient for entertainment for many years. The various church congregations were, of course, larger but all seem to have had clubs and events attached to them. Dances in the Town Hall and the Norton Club were extremely popular and the highlight of many peoples week. The cinema was widely patronised and a change of programme at least twice weekly was the norm. Sports were widely enjoyed; football, cricket and, of course, baseball, were participated in by many residents. All these interests were pursued by both old and young alike who seemed to enjoy each other's company in their leisure activities more readily than one would find nowadays.

Chipping Norton is lucky, and also fairly unique, in having photographs taken by Percy Simms and Frank and Basil Packer that are not only extensive in their subject matter but also survive in enormous numbers. Many are lodged with the Photographic Archives in the Centre for Oxfordshire Studies and many are with the Chipping Norton Historical Society; all give a wonderful recollection of life and social history during a large part of the twentieth century. There have, as those interested in Chipping Norton and its history know, been several other interesting books on this town and this book seeks to complement them. Endeavours have been made to capture here, not only photographs but the names of those so encapsulated and their memories of Chipping Norton. In compiling any book in this series one is dependent on the frailty of human memory in recalling names, events and dates. Whilst every care has been taken to ensure the facts are as accurate as possible, it should be remembered that by using this source rather than documented events errors can on occasions occur; corrections can be made, if notified, in a reprint at a later date. With the wealth of material available, a second book in the series is planned and the author would be pleased to hear from anyone with photogpraphs or other relevant material.

Employment

In 1899 there was a serious fire at Simms, the jewellers which also affected Morrisons, the cycle agent and repair firm. Access to Black Boy Yard, also known as Simms Yard, which ran from the High Street up to Back lane, now Albion Street, was via the archway seen in the photograph. Near the top of the yard were six cottages; some of these were already in poor condition so after the fire Mr Simms decided to demolish them. A house and shop were built in place of the two shops which had been destroyed. The entrance to the yard from Back Lane was under an archway formed by a whale's jaw bones; it is not known when these disappeared.

The two photographs above show the interior and exterior damage to Simms shop. (A. Brain)

A view from Black Boy Yard, which led from High Street to Albion Street, showing repairs being undertaken. (A. Brain)

Taken outside Webb's department store on Hospital Saturday in 1912. Left to right: ?, Nan Harris (married Sid Stanley), Mrs Norman Rowell, Beatrice Victoria Hannis (nee Clark), Miss Brice, Mrs Medley.

Webb's shop. As their sign shows, this family business sold knitwear, costumes, skirts, dresses, coats, ladies and childrenswear. The firm had a couple of vans to make deliveries to the local area. In the late 1930s the starting wage for working in the office was 5 shillings per week rising by half a crown after six months. The Webb family originally came to Chipping Norton as weavers in the Bliss Mill c 1756; early members of the family were Baptists. The first shop at 16 New Street was a grocer, draper, upholsterer and furniture dealer. Later A.A. Webb purchased Nos: 11, 12, 13 and 16 Market Place, the shop occupying Nos: 12-13. Until 1918 the firm had resident staff who lived in. The shop hours were standard for the time: 8am to 7 pm Monday to Saturday and 8am to 9pm on Saturdays.

Taken c1920, this photograph shows haymaking possibly in the Lewis Road area. Third from the left is Ernie Johnston.

Haymaking at Meades Farm c1936, Mrs Tipping and Mrs Florence Honour.

Kecks at 20 High Street, c1890s. The Keck family owned this business from the eighteenth to the start of the twentieth century. In 1800 Thomas Keck was listed as a Rope Merchant and a Rag and Bone Merchant, by 1901 Putmans advertised cycles, sports dealers and tents for hire. Mr Keck is presumably the figure in the shop doorway; there appear to be a wide variety of goods available, rope, broom and mop heads, for example. When making an especially long rope, a rope walk was set up from the top of Middle Row gardens, across High Street and through the garden to Albion Street and to the top of the Foundry Yard. Twisting began and by 8am the rope stretched from the edge of High Street to the edge of Albion Street. (A. Brain).

Mr Freeman was a well known hairdresser in Middle Row. (A. Brain) In the 1920s there were two other barbers in the town, Mr Willets and Mr Witts.

Blisss Tweed Mill Group c 1910. Left to right: James Brain, ?, Mr Herbert. (A. Brain)

Hartwells the ironmongers, 19 High Street, was owned by John Hartwell. The premises were used as ironmongers over a long period; the proprietors were: 1870 Henry Dashwood, 1891 G. Padbury followed by a Mr Slipper, then John Hartwell.

Before World War II, when Harry Powers was the landlord of the Brewers Arms in Albion Street, boys would take empty screw top bottles from the pub yard, half fill them with water and add a handful of carbide purchased from Hartwells. They would then take them to the builders yard in Wards Road, screw the tops on and throw them; the bottles would explode like a bomb. Unfortunately one once failed to explode and the unlucky volunteer bent on retrieving it was left with a piece of glass embedded in his forehead. Nowadays this would have required stitches but on reporting for work the next day looking decidedly the worse for wear, the victim was dispatched to Boots the Chemist and a layer of Friars Balsam was spread on the wound; he lived to tell the tale.

Rocky Leach

Henry Thomas Leach jnr was born in Rugby in 1900 and the family moved to Banbury where Henry Thomas Leach snr, known as 'Rocky Tom' had a sweet making business, most of which was carried on in the market. He also owned several properties and let one to his son who, wanting to get into the business, sold a few of his own sweets from the house: Henry snr thought this was opposition. Henry jnr had married Lillian Matilda Edwards from Wales and when she inherited a small legacy the couple decided to move to Chipping Norton. They bought the building, originally owned by Minchins, and subsequently by Robinsons, the greengrocers c1934 for £600. In the early days 'Rocky' Leach, as he became known, made rock and sweets in an alleyway alongside Rowells; he also rented a workshop in Distons Lane. In c1936/37 he rented other premises along Horsefair directly opposite the doctor's surgery.

Once war broke out and rationing was introduced, the business declined because there was not the sugar available to make the sweets. It became necessary for 'Rocky' Leach to get a part time job on the railway, unfortunately in 1945 he fell off a truck and was off work for a few days. Starting back at his own employment before he should have done Mr Leach suffered a severe accident. He had just poured 56lb of boiling sugar onto a slab when he felt giddy and fell forward into the bubbling mass. His son, Les Leach, was with him and pulled him out but he was not strong enough to support his fathers weight so that Mr Leach fell and hit his head on the slab. Les poured water on his father and ran across to the doctor's surgery. Mr Leach was rushed to Chipping Norton hospital by ambulance, but he died a few weeks later.

Les Leach carried on serving in the shop and making a few sweets for about twelve months, but his mother was always worried there might be another accident. She remarried and the business was sold.

'Rocky' Leach sold boiled sweets, bullseyes and pear drops being the main ones. The rock was strawberry flavoured and coloured with a cross inside, or peppermint (brown) with a grid pattern inside. It was always square, metal bars being used to give the correct shape after it had been drawn out by hand. 'Rocky' would make special orders to suit, lemon and lime and a rock where the middle showed a strawberry complete with pips and leaves. He sometimes made fudge and experimented with chocolate.

'Rocky' also made ice cream which he called creamed ice and he would only make this with goat's milk. This was because at this time cows were commonly T.B. infected and, in Mr Leach's estimation, if one ate three or four ice creams made from cows milk a week it was possible to infect oneself. Goats milk was T.B. free and so there was no risk.

Another sideline was fizzy drinks; a copper bottle with a rocker was set up and gas was introduced into the mixture. The container was then rocked to spread the bubbles evenly.

'Rocky' made a special potion when his family were unwell. It included paragarrig (an essence), syrup of squills and peppermint and the resulting drink warmed as it was swallowed; the family called it Johnick.

In this photograph 'Rocky' Leach's premises can be seen between the Bunch of Grapes and Ivy House. Ivy House was run by Miss FitzGibbon and her brother who were reputedly either Irish Catholics or Jewish. The shop sold everything, except furniture, at a reasonable price.

The window on the first floor of Mr Leach's premises was the lounge and above that was Mr and Mrs Leach's bedroom. The attic room above was occupied by Molly Tanner, daughter of the Great Rollright cobbler, who was the Leach's nanny.

As a child Les Leach used to climb into the gully between the buildings, sometimes with a friend. He laid boards across the gully and made it into a 'den' where he could play and have picnics. One evening when he was rather adventurous, he peeped into a skylight at the Bunch of Grapes and, after a report from the couple occupying the room, a policeman was dispatched to have words!

Below the shop was an underground kitchen, beneath that a cellar and beneath that yet another cellar. This one had a well in it which was probably about 20 foot deep with an ancient pump. There was also a trough carved from a block of granite. In this cellar there was an archway about 4 foot high which went about 30 foot in before it ended; the bricks here were all cut to shape. 'Rocky' Leach had the well filled with ashes and the bottom cellar was filled in.

The premises of Shrimpton, baker, grocer and provision merchant at the corner of New Street and Market Place. Cadburys chocolate was presumably as popular then as it is now!

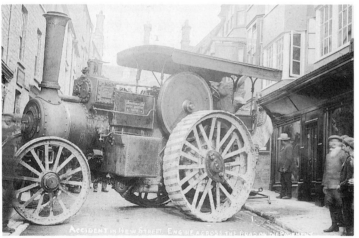

Prior to demolition New Street was notoriously narrow as this photograph of a Hook Norton steamroller shows. (A. Brain)

After the railway opened in 1854 the traffic in New Street increased and it was decided to increase the width from 24 feet to 34 feet in the lower part. Unfortunately the top part was left as there were insufficient funds available to purchase the necessary properties for demolition, hence the resulting congestion.

11 Market Place prior to demolition, it was occupied in 1945 by Bignells as a cafe as well as bakers and confectioners.

The demolition at the top of New Street. These two photographs were taken in October, 1977.

Photographed at the Co-op bakery, left to right: Jess Hadland, Bob Moulder, Fred Brooks and Harry Tidmarsh the Foreman c 1920. Deliveries were made to the surrounding villages and the baker would also deliver clothes that were sent out 'on appro'.

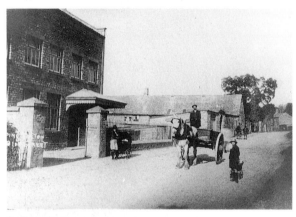

The Co-operative bakery photographed from Albion Street.

The Co-op butchers in West Street. Left to right: Ben Hovard, Cyril Smart snr, Jim Shepard, Bill Fiddler, George Withers, George Beard, Mr Haynes, Frank Jarvis. The Co-op had their own slaughter-house: gammons were wrapped in brown paper and hung on hooks after they had been salted in brine and covered in brown sugar; when the maggots fell out they were ready to eat.

The Co-op butchers c 1950. Left to right: Mr Hines, Jim Shepherd, George Beard. (R. Stares).

Co-op boots, shoes and mens outfitters. Left to right: Cyril Withers, Ken Wallington, Mr Horwood (The Manager), Minnie Smart (nee Parsons), Bill Thornton, Richard Moulder and Eric Hoare.

'The Chipping Norton Co-op were a high-class department store. Its Diamond Jubilee in 1926 were a tremendous occasion. Chippy were choc-a-bloc. Every-body in their best Co-op suit and Sunday hat. A first Co-op Sunday suit 'ud see a young man well into middle life, a second 'ud see him out, not exactly fitting but still respectable, at a ripe old age'. (Mont Abbot, *Lifting the Latch* by Sheila Stewart, Oxford University Press)

Cyril Smart snr with the Co-operative Society van. (A. Brain)

Mr Howerd Harding with the last Co-op horse, 26 August 1957. (A. Brain). When Mr Harding had finished his deliveries, which were often outside the town as far as the Rollright Stones, he said 'Gee up' to the horse and dozed whilst the horse took him safely back to the yard. Although Mr Harding is photographed here it was Dick Turner who had the last horse.

Hartwell and Barlows garage in 1928.

According to a advertisement in a local newspaper, Hartwells garage was 'developed from an existing business in Chipping Norton, the present garage being opened in 1913'. By 1920 a directory contains the information that Hartwell Rollright Limited, trading as Hartroll, was situated in Horsefair. The directors at this time were A.R. Hartwell, P.S. Robinson, R.A. Young and H.N. Barlow. Sometime between this date and 1928 the garage changed to Hartwell and Barlow (telephone No: 41); by 1931 the name was again changed to G.R. Hartwell Ltd. Mr Barlow was an ironmonger by trade and it is believed he learned about motor vehicles during World War I; certainly his association with the motor industry was short lived, due probably to a falling out, and he moved to Banbury and his original occupation.

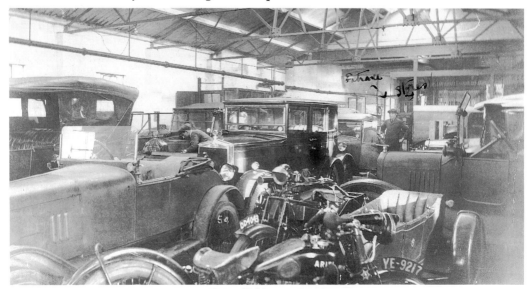

The interior of the garage in 1928.

The Hannis family

Charles William Hannis (b1854) was apprenticed to Mr Belcher who had a tailoring business in the High Street. He ran off to Aldershot and enlisted in the 17th Foot under the name of William Hannis and was placed in the regimental band and taught the cornet for which he showed great aptitude. After almost two years his mother discovered his whereabouts and took him back to Chipping Norton and Mr Belcher. Although he did run away again, eventually he did return and bought a tailoring business from Mr Castle and moved the business to the Old Guildhall in Middle Row. He also bought Mr Belcher's business in High Street c1920; by this time it had passed to Martin Walsh.

C. W. Hannis started a tailor's business at Bourton on the Water, travelling to customers in a pony and cart and later by car. He set his second wife, Clara Bailey, up in a drapery business at Bourton on the Water which was carried on by his daughter Beatrice May Hannis after Clara's death in 1916 whilst she was mayoress. When Beatrice died in 1918 during the flu epidemic the business was carried on by Frank Hannis. C. W. Hannis was one of the founders of Chipping Norton Ratepayers' Association which had its headquarters in the Blue Boar. He was involved with the town council for many years including terms as Alderman and Mayor. For many years he was bandmaster of Chipping Norton Volunteer Band and had a string band of his own which was popular for dances.

George Henry Hannis had served during World War I and had been apprenticed to his father. When C. W. Hannis died in 1935 G.H. Hannis carried on the business. He did the cutting and in addition there were 4 employees, 2 tailors who worked on the premises and 2 ladies, Violet Castle and Sarah Hands. In the early days there were lots of good tailors who wouldn't stay in one place for too long, but would work for two or three months before they moved on, often returning some months later. These men lodged at The Chequers in Spring Street and were often ex-army men. The tailors sat on a raised platform cross legged to do their sewing, even in the mid 1950s. There was also a treadle sewing machine. A huge table to press the garments on was another fixture. The firms customers were varied; farmers who paid their bills once a year (they were supposed to), the aristocracy, the Heythrop Hunt kennels and most of the large local estates such as Blenheim and Ditchley.

G. H. Hannis was a founder member of the local golf club and also founded the local fire brigade charity with funds from the sale of the town's own fire engine when it was taken over by the local authority. He was a member of the Chipping Norton Town side which won the Oxfordshire Senior League in 1912 and was President of the Oxfordshire F.A from 1957 until c1967. He served as a borough councillor for many years and was also mayor, retiring as Alderman in 1960 when he gave up the business.

"It were a small genteel establishment, stuffed with quality, from its thick mahogany counter to its new silent electric light. The sporty looking tweed-suited proprietor and his quietly dressed lady assistant looked up in surprise as I stood at the opened door, not wanting to cart in all the mud on my working clobber...

'How much for a bespoke suit for the likes of me'?

'It depends on the cloth, Sir, – and the amount' he added, sizing up my workday frame propping open his mahogany doorway. 'A good wool worsted for you, Sir, woven at our local mill, would be £18...'

I can still recall the shared excitement of choosing my first tweed with Mr Hannis, flopping out all they quality cloths on the rich polished counter. It were to be the first of four best suits threading my life to him, and then to his son, over the next thirty years ... Old Mr Hannis made it in three weeks; he felt beholden, he said, having been paid prior, to give me priority." (Mont Abbot in *Lifting the Latch,* by Sheila Stewart, Oxford University Press)

C.W. Hannis with his sons, February 1916. Left to right back row: George Hannis, Frank Hannis and Bill Hannis who lost an arm during World War I. Front row: C.W. Hannis and Fred Hannis.

The shop was at 10 High Street. It is perported that once a sheep was sheared in the morning, the wool spun and woven into cloth and a hunting jacket made by Mr Hannis by nightfall.

Outside Hitchman's head office; off sales were available here. In 1796 William Spence Hitchman founded the brewery which was incorporated in 1890 as brewers, maltsers, licensed victuallers, mineral water manufacturers, hotelkeepers, restaurant, wine, spirit, tobacco and hop and coal merchants. At that time the Company had 24 freehold licensed houses, 12 leasehold houses and malt houses producing 8,000 grams of malt per annum. In the 1930s it was possible to get 1 pint of beer, a packet of woodbines and a sleeve of matches from the pubs for 6d.

Lorries in the Hitchmans Brewery yard, the men are left to right: Mr Waring, Joby Townley, ?, Michael Kite, ?, ?, ?, Mr Caswell, ?, Harry Kite.

Henry Margetts, c 1930s at the Cleves. Mr Margetts was cowman for Freddy Warmington.

Dr Kelly with his son-in-law Dr Russell. Dr Kelly was the first doctor to have a car in Chipping Norton.

During World War II a plane crashed onto Dr Russell's garage. He climbed out of the skylight in his pyjamas with his medical bag to try and reach the plane. A large explosion threw him back onto the roof but he persisted and got onto and into the plane and rescued the pilot, although there were some casualties.

Making bread deliveries in Guildhall Place before World War II. (A. Brain) The men are Co-op employees and are left to right: Leonard Bench, Ernie Jarvis and ?. This was the only house in Guildhall Place that had a bow window, and its occupant, Mrs Hepburn, is standing in the doorway. The lady on the left is probably Mrs Abbott.

The window of Mr and Mrs Hepburn's house with a display of papers and magazines, August 1930 (A. Brain).

Mr Hepburn on the left is selling newspapers at 'The Shed' c1935/56; Mrs Hepburn is standing behind the counter and third from the right is Ray Swan.

Inside Hubbs Ironworks in the early 1950s. Left to right: Fred Panting, Arthur Fletcher, Frank Roper.

Another view inside the ironworks, the employees unidentified. (A. Brain)

Below: 19 West End was owned from c1850 by one family. At one time the last building in the Borough except for the pest house, it was for a time the New Inn; Mr Smith kept the premises as an off licence for many years. Mary Jane Lane inherited the property in 1914; reputedly a staunch teetotaller it is commonly believed she kept a general shop instead. However, documentary evidence exists to show that she placed orders with Hitchmans brewers. She kept a small account book for those who couldn't pay.

Miss Burden ran the Bon Marche in West Street which sold bits and bobs. China, wrapped in newspaper and packed in an old fashioned clothes basket, could be hired as well as a tea urn for special occasions. The shop had closed by the early 1950s.

John Hannis c1960.

John worked for Pettipher & Sons making deliveries to the surrounding villages: licensing laws used to be strict and it was not possible to purchase alcohol from them between 12 and 2pm; however, if it was delivered to one's house or car this was all right. He then worked for Mr Webb on his farm for a while where work was done by horses and cows were milked by hand before joining Walter Craft & Son. They were corn and seed merchants and had a mill by the station .

John returned here after a spell in the army before joining the bus company as a driver; he stayed there 46 years. He drove the bus from Chipping Norton to Oxford via Great Tew, Middle Barton, Steeple Aston, Rousham and Kidlington. The bus garage used to be in Albion Street next to Hub Ironworks which was owned by the Rowell family and was a large employer. At its busiest there were two double decker buses, each holding 52 people, each day to Morris Motors in Oxford. The garage then moved to the London Road where it remained until c1985 when it closed and the premises were taken over by Parker Knoll, although buses are still parked here.

There was a bus run some years earlier by a private company; it was called Safety First and a return to Oxford was 1s 6d. Jack Sims had a coach in which he used to take the Salvation Army Band to its various venues around the villages; the charge was 1s per person per day. After 1935 it was possible for the Band to hire the City of Oxford coach on a Sunday morning for £1 to go wherever they wanted.

The Cacti Cafe on the site of the former International Stores, with Vic and Madge Cooper and their son in the late 1960s. Vic's first cafe was in New Street where Fosters first had their premises. (R. Stares).

Refurbishing the Church of England Boys School for the vicarage in the late 1960s. (R. Stares).

The opening of the International Stores in 1981; the manager Angus Stephen with the winner of the rabbit.

The Market

Permission to hold fairs was granted in 1205 and from this grew the twice weekly market, and the monthly cattle market held on Wednesdays. In addition Hiring Fairs or Mops were held on three consecutive Wednesdays in October although these had died out in the early 1900s. The location for the Hiring Fairs was the Town Hall, the women sitting inside on forms and the men standing outside, each with the emblem of their trades. In 1890 the average age of the girls was 11 and the pay was 1s per week whilst the men received between 4s and 7s per week.

In the last years of the nineteenth century, an Indian gentleman named Mr Sequora came to Chipping Norton on market days together with two or three men with cornets. His claim that he could extract teeth painlessly was supported by these men playing very loudly to drown the customers' screams.

From the mid 1800s an amusement fair was held at the time of the Hiring Fairs, and although this gradually ceased, the custom was revived in 1930 when Hubert Packer was mayor. Celebrations held included an Ox roast, the meat being sold at 1s 6d per plate. The dates for this fair were the third Thursday, Friday and Saturday of September and is still retained as the 'Chippy Mop'.

'I remember Chippy Mop when I was 8 or 9 (c1890). There were roundabouts and swinging boats on the bank, up each side of the road were stalls, toys, sweets, vans, a fortune teller, a fat lady, dwarfs who had a son 6 foot tall, a tent where a horse had his tail where his head should have been, baked potatoes and chestnuts and a man with a sausage stall which he cooked crying out 'sausages and bread 1d, warm your hand and fill your belly'. (Women's Institute records)

Dix's lorry sunk into a cellar in Market Street in the mid 1950s. Left to right; Tom Dix, ? Thornton, John Smart, ?. (A. Brain)

Work on Chipping Norton's war memorial. (A. Brain)

Religion and Education

Photographed at the Band of Hope Festival in 1914, it is not known what happened to the banner. (A. Brain)

The Band of Hope was founded in Chipping Norton by Mr Roles, Mr D.R. Simms and Mr Willie Burbidge in the early 1880s. This was in response to the large number of drunks of both sexes amongst the workers involved in the construction of the tunnel. Within a very short while over 400 members had enrolled and recitations and singing evenings, all with an anti alcohol theme, were very popular. In 1883 a Blue Ribbon Mission, held at the Town Hall with all seats taken, resulted in 316 pledges and 719 Blue Ribbons. The Band of Hope was a non-conformist organisation with two members from the Primitive Methodist, Baptist, Methodist and Wesleyan Churches in charge.

Another helper was Sergeant Russell. The gentleman at the back of the above photograph, with his hand against the banner, is possibly Mr Kitchen from Burford Terrace who was a keen member.

An early, possibly private, school group Left to right front row: Miss Bound, M. Mace, H. Jeffries. Middle row: Ernest Barlow, E. Simms, C. Jeffries. Back row: H. Barlow, Muriel Barlow, I.G. Mace and B. Simms.

The Salvation Army

When the Salvation Army came to Chipping Norton at the end of March, 1887 Captain McFetrick wrote 'We have opened fire on this town in right good earnest. Our barracks, which is a club room connected to a public house, is filled every night. On Sunday afternoon, we were packed out and had an overflow meeting in the market square, attended by over four hundred people.' Between March and September of 1887 the Salvation Army congregation increased and the local publicans realised that they were losing some of their customers. Subsequently the Army found themselves holding services in a field in Albion Street which belonged to Mr Hamblett of the Fox Hotel.

In the following six months serious opposition to the work of the Salvation Army developed in the town so that the following report appeared in the Army's newspaper *War Cry* on 31 March, 1888. 'We have received information of an outstanding nature regarding organised and systematic opposition to our open-air work in Chipping Norton. We are informed that not only are male soldiers kicked and beaten during the whole of the time they are making their way to their barracks, but the same treatment is extended to women. Night after night, these lasses, in passing up the narrow lane, have to run the gauntlets of blows, kicks, obscene language and even indecent assaults.'

The matter of these assaults was raised in the House of Commons when it was mentioned that the Chief Constable had too few constables to protect the Salvationists against attacks from the gang of persons who called themselves the Skeleton Army. A special correspondent, a Mr Longfellow, was sent to Chipping Norton to take first hand interviews of alleged opposition and harassment. His investigations revealed that during the year the army had been operating in the vicinity, some so-called 'dancing rooms' had

closed, pubs had emptied, some of the more desperate characters of the town converted and a Salvation Army Corps of more than one hundred soldiers had been formed. One publican revealed that his takings had gone down considerably since the Army came to the town and one convert who had been a heavy drinker in that pub said that with the money he had saved on drink he had purchased two pigs!

Eventually the Home Office intervened and Salvationists were allowed to march freely and hold their open-air services without fear of physical attack. Money was raised and on 3 August 1888 a stone-laying ceremony was held for the beginning of their new building. Commandant Herbert Booth, the third son of the founder William Booth, attended and a thanksgiving meeting was held in the Town Hall. Four months later Miss Evangeline Booth arrived and on the Sunday evening both the new Salvation Army Hall and the Town Hall were filled to capacity and many could not get in.

Outside the Salvation Army Hall c1936. Left to right Captain and Mrs Wright, Mrs Benfield, Joe Tanner, ?. It has not been possible to identify the children.

Salvation Army Band in 1930, one year old (Alan Brain). Left to right front row: Reggie Benfield, Victor Harris. First row: Captain Latham, Bill Townley (Bandmaster), Lieutenant Hastings, John Benfield (drum). Back row: George Cross, Thomas Pickett, Jim Pickett, Sydney Dee, George Withers, Harry Pickett, Phil Harris, Nobby Clarke. (Alan Brain). The band was commissioned on Easter Sunday.

Salvation Army Corps c1929 with the Northampton Division Commander. Left to right back row: Phil Harris, Bill Townley, Jim Pickett, Harry Pickett, Thomas Pickett, George Cross, Les Fawdry (from Jericho Gardens), Nobby Clark, Sidney Dee, John Benfield. Second row: Joe Tanner, Mark Holifield, George Withers, Mrs Siggers (the young persons' Sergeant Major), Edie Cross, Mrs Benfield, Fred Heath, Albert Pratt, Chris Cooper. Third row: Mrs Fewster, Staff-Captain Fewster, Brigadier Lean, Captain Latham, Lieutenant Hastings. Front row: Henry ? (Regs cousin), Les Pickett, Dick Harris, Muriel Pickett, Reggie Benfield.

It was quite common for bands from other areas to visit Chipping Norton, as in this photograph. This is not the complete band, just a part of it. (Alan Brain)

Inside the Salvation Army Hall c1931, Captain Will Hutchinson on the left and Lieutenant Strahan on the right. (Alan Brain)

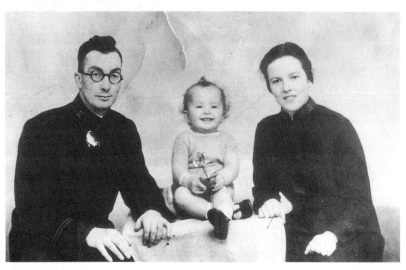

Captain and Mrs H. Wright and their son John in 1940.

Sadly in 1962 the Salvation Army closed its doors in Chipping Norton. The cost of building the hall was £887 12s 9d; it was sold in February 1970 for £1,550.

The Methodist Church Japanese Bazaar, February 1933. Left to right front row: ?, ?, Mrs Rutten. On the far right is the Rev. Owen who married the lady on the far left. Middle row: ?, ?, ?, ?, Mrs Woodcock (her husband worked in Hartwell's general shop), Miss Bunn (schoolteacher at Penhurst who lived over the common with her mother and later moved to Chipping Norton), Mrs Newman (from Salford), Mrs Hobbs (from Chadlington). Back row: ?, ?, Lily Senear (nee Tipping), Mrs Tidmarsh, Harry Tidmarsh, Mrs Lane (owned a general and sweet shop in West Street), ?, ?, Sister Dorothy Ford (with hat), third from the right is Mr Lane.

Photographed c1950 in the Town Hall during the 'Bright Hour'. This took place on Thursday afternoon when older folk went along around 3pm for a talk and cup of tea. The second lady on the right in the flowered apron is Mrs Tipping and next to her is Mr Tipping, on Mrs Tipping's other side is Mrs Burden. Between them in the back row is Sister Dorothy Ford and, on the far right Mrs Randall whose husband worked in Brindles.

St Mary's Church Choir in the early 1940s. Left to right, back row: Mr Candy, Les Slade, Ernest Barnes, Mr Bolter, Leslie Smart, Angus Stephen, Frank Jarvis, ?, Mr Hill, Mr Pettipher, Mr Moore, Dennis Jarvis, at the end of the ladies is Michael Moore. The ladies are: ?, Mrs Croft, ?, Mrs Perry, D. Willets, M. Barnes. The man with the glasses next to Rev. Thomas is Mr Rose and D. Barnes is on the vicar's other side. The last two boys on the right are C. Smart and Jack Tanner.

St Mary's Church choir in the mid 1940s. Left to right, back row: Frank Jarvis, Ernie Barnes, ?, ?, Mr Boulter, D. Barnes, M. Moore. Second row: Mr Hill, Mr Pettipher, Mr Hutchinson, L. Slade, Dennis Tidmarsh, Rev. Thomas,?, F. Barnes, D. Jarvis, Angus Stephen, ?, ?, D. Willets, ?. The ladies are: Mrs Croft, Mrs Perry, M. Willetts and M. Barnes. The boys are unknown.

Chipping Norton Boys School c1905. Middle row 3rd from left is Albert Brain (b 1895) and 6th from left is Les Burbidge. The teacher is Mr Ralph "Gaffer" Oakes.

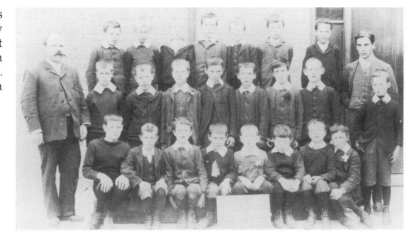

Chipping Norton Grammar School c 1938. Left to right back row: Dorothy Clare, Margaret Downes, Margaret Woolcock, Mary Stayte. Middle row: Dorothy Sandall, Joan Mason, Maureen Coram, Nancy Absolam, Evadne Crow. Front row: Mae Goss, Barbara Morris, Freda Hudson. Maureen Corams father, Harold, was the accountant at Bliss Mill in the 1920s.

School group 1931. Left to right top row: Penhurst girl, ?, Phyllis Fisher, ?,?, ? Aries (Over Norton). Second row: Beryl Packer, Noreen Smith, Olive Moulder, Molly Mason, ?, Nancy ?. Third row: Annie Tipping, Penhurst girl, Penhurst girl, Janet Sanders, June Blakey, Doris Brown, Dorothy Fisher, ? Calcutt. Front row: Margaret Stradbolt, Jean Harris, Joan Gibbard, Lily Keen, Barbara Honour, Kath Pratt, ?, Eva Naylor.

Chipping Norton Infants' School, c1949. Left to right front row: ?, ?, Janet Keen, Marilyn Hill, Jean Harris, ?, ?, ?, Jennifer Stevens, Ann Rogers. Middle row: ?, ?, ?, ?, ?, ?, ?, ?, ?, ?, ?. Back row: ?, ?, Michael Gibbard, ?, Rodney Harding, ?, ?, Donald Branson, ?.

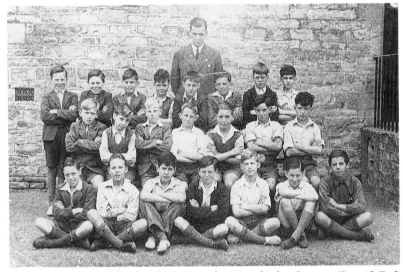

The Church of England Boys' School 1949. Left to right back row: David Roberts, Pete Day, Brian Powers, Kenny Berry, Terry Cox, Brian Allen, Ivor Howse, Alan Watkins. Middle row: Michael Goodman, Pete Watts, Bruce Durno, Syd Bailey, Peter Bridges, Tony Pick, Les Walton. Front row: John Grantham, David Clarke, Paul Ashmore, Edward Price, Peter Johnson, Peter Clacy, Gilbert Clifton. The teacher is Mr Wykes.

A group of Chipping Norton Grammar School boys in 1953. Left to right: Malcolm Smith (Charlbury), Bob Butler (Enstone), Edward Green (Chilson), Michael Groves (Stonesfield), John Betteridge (Chadlington).

Chipping Norton Grammar School chess team 1952. Left to right, back row: Mr Miles, Ron Baughan, ? Payne, ? Allen. Front row: John Grantham, ? Claridge, ? Edgington.

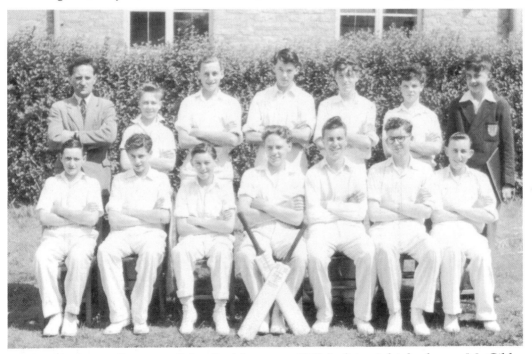

Chipping Norton Grammar School cricket team 1952. Left to right, back row: Mr Gibbs, Pete Frame, Ron Baughan, John Kinch, John Grantham, Kenny Berry, ? Harding. Front row: ? Mason, Graham Taplin, Tony Downer, David Clark, Keith Vickers, ? Claridge, Brian Davis.

Chipping Norton Co-operative Society Limited (A. R. Chance, sec.); registered office, 4 High st ; Market pl. ; Albion st. & West st.   T A " Co-operative ; " T N 3

Chipping Norton & District War Memorial Hospital (Miss M. M. Joslin, sec.) ; Miss Dorothy Pashley, matron), Over Norton rd.   T N 16

Chipping Norton Electric Supply Co. Limited, Burford road.   T N 46

Chipping Norton Gas Light & Coke Co. Ltd. (P. S. Shepherd, manager & sec.), 12 West st

Chipping Norton Picture House (T. W. Grant, manager), London rd.   T N 9

Chipping Norton Social Club (E. Townsend, sec.), 20 West st

Church Army Social Centre (Capt. Fred Read), New st

Constable Mary (Mrs.), fishmngr. 7 New st.   T N 19

Corner Café (H. Bigwell, propr.), 11 Market pl.   T N 103

County Court (His Honour Digby Cotes-Preedy K.C. judge; Edwd. Claude Fortescue, registrar & high bailiff)

Craft Walter & Sons Ltd. corn & seed merchants, 6 & 7 Market place.   T N 66

Crosfield Paul M.A., M.R.C.V.S. veterinary surgn. & inspector to the Ministry of Agriculture, Glovers close, Albion st.   T N 47

Crown Hotel, family & commercial (Sydney Hall, propr.), High street.   T N's 33 & 121

Customs & Excise Office (Wltr. Hy. Arrowsmith, officer) (attends wed. 2 to 4 p.m.), London rd

Digwood Owen Jas. farmer, Rockhill farm, London rd

Dring Thos. shopkpr. London rd

Duncan Thos. fried fish dlr. 2 Middle row

Durham & Giles (H. A. Giles), boot dlrs. 17 High st. T N 67

Eastmans Limited, butchers, 3 Middle row

Farrant Sidney Geo. solctr & commissioner for oaths & clerk to commissioners of taxes Chadlington district & clerk to Chipping Norton county magistrates, 1 High st.   T N 15

Ferriman Chas. Steven Haynes, house decrtr. 3a, Churchill rd

Fire Brigade, West st

Fortescue Edwd. C. solctr. & commissioner for oaths (firm, Stockton, Sons & Fortescue), clerk to the county magistrates & registrar & high bailiff of county court, 10 Market pl.   T N 40

Foster Bros. Clothing Co. Ltd. outfitters, 3 New st

Fox P.H. (Lionel Jn. Shenstone), 2 Market pl.   T N 158

Fox & Hounds P.H. (Geo. Florey), Worcester rd

Freeborn Geo. Arth. & Son, butchers, 20 Market pl.   T N 25

Freeman Bert, tobccnst. 8 Middle row.   T N 68

Frost Bernard T. coal & coke mer. Station yard

George P.H. (Mrs. Florence M. Hovard), 4 New st

Good Luck Café (Mrs. Edginton), 12 High st

Goodwin & Cuthbert, butchers, 11 New st.   T N 38

Green Wm. supt. of police & inspector under the Explosives, Shop Hours & Diseases of Animals Acts, Police station, London rd.   T N 8

Guy Jsph. shopkpr. 25 Worcester rd

Hannis Geo. Hy. tailor, 10 High st.   T N 50

Hardy Geoffrey, insur. agt. Wendover-Norton rd

Harris Alice Mary (Mrs.), costumier, 59 New st

Harris Florence Eliza (Miss), district nurse, 35 West end

Hartwell G. R. Ltd. motor car agts. Horsefair.   T N 41

Hartwell's (Norman Galloway), ironmngrs. 19 High st. T N 35

Hearn Ernest Edwd. confctnr. 16 New st

Hearts of Oak Benefit Society (F. H. Hall, agt.), 3 West End

Hebborn Frank, newsagt. 1 Guildhall pl

Hewett G. F. & Son, grocers, 9 Middle row

Heythrop Hounds (Lord Ashton of Hyde, master ; Percy Durno, huntsman), The Kennels, Worcester rd. T N 52

Hilton Stephen & Sons Ltd. boot & shoe retlrs. 24 High st

Hitchman & Co. Limited (associated with Hunt, Edmunds & Co. Ltd.), **brewers, wine & spirit merchants & aerated water manufacturers, West street. Telephone 5**

Hutton, auctioneer, land, house & estate agent & surveyor, 25 High st.   T N 177.   **See Advt. Index**

International Tea Co.'s Stores Limited, tea mers. 17 Market pl.   T N 31

James Edwin, baker, 50 West st

Jarvis Jas. Hy. chimney sweeper, 31 Rock hill

Jeffries J. W. & Sons, coal & coke merchants, 34 New street & at Railway Station yard.   T N 172

Johnston Ernest Fredk. Wm. boot repr. 6 West st

Kenyon Edwd. rating & valuation officer, clerk to Chipping Norton Rural District Council & supt. registrar Chipping Norton district, 16a, Market pl.   T N 21

King's Arms P.H. (W. A. Barber), 18 West st

Kite Mrs. boarding ho. 16 Market pl

Lane Mary (Mrs.), shopkeeper, 19 West end

Langton Herbt. Harold, refrshmnt. rms. 10 New st

Leach Hy. Thos. confctnr. 23 Market pl

Lewis Fred, bldr. 5 Market st.   T N 73

London Central Meat Co. Ltd. butchers, 6 High st

Lord Jn. Edwd. baker, 30 High st.   T N 61

Masonic Lodge (The Bowyer, 2,036) (Oswald Leonard Carrington, secretary), Masonic temple, Over Norton road

Mealin Thos. blacksmith, 31 Albion st

Mellor Rhubert William Henry M.A.Oxon. surveyor to Oxford County Council, Chipping Norton division, Banbury rd.   T N 102

Midland Bank Ltd. (Bertram Brookbanks, mngr.) (10 a.m. till 3 p.m. ; sat 9 a.m. till 12 noon), Market pl. (T N 37) ; head office, Poultry, London E C 2

Miles L. B. draper, Market pl.   T N 27

Ministry of Labour Employment Exchange (D. C. Davis, manager), Friends Meeting house. New st.   T N 75

Morris Frank Wm. town clerk & clerk to Chipping Norton Sub-Committee of Oxfordshire Local Pension Committee, to the burial board & Urban District Council, 10 Market pl.   T N 53

Mott Geo. motor engnr. West End garage, West st. T N 62

Mullis Ernest Denis, confctnr. 9 Horsefair

National Children's Home & Orphanage (The) (Miss Little, matron), New st.   T N 59

National Farmers' Union

Naylor Norman, ladies' hairdrssr. 33 West st.   T N 138

New Cinema (Chipping Norton) Ltd. New st.   T N 141

Nicholls Ethel Ruth (Mrs.), fancy repository, 31 High st

Nock N. J., L.D.S.Birm. dental surgn. (firm, Robinson & Nock) (attends tues. wed. & fri.), 26 High st. TN 61

Oddfellows (No. 5,864) (Manchester Unity, Banbury district) (J. J. Marshall, sec.), London rd

O'Shea Jn. Patrick M.R.C.S., L.R.C.P. physcn. & surgn. Manor ho. West st

Oxford County Council (Chipping Norton divisional surveyor's office ; Rhubert William Henry Mellor M.A. Oxon. surveyor), Banbury rd.   T N 102

Oxford House P.H. (J. W. F. Scrivener), 18 Horsefair

Packer Fras. Rd. photographer, 28 High st.   T N 76

Parrot Inn (Percy Goodwin), Market st

Partridge Thos. poultry farmer, Worcester rd

Pauling Howard Thos. dairy farmer, West End farm, 43 West st.   T N 120

°Pauling Leonard W. farmer, Meads farm

Pearce Fred, chemist, 8 High st.   T N 127

Pearl Assurance Co. Ltd. (Frank Downing, district manager), 11 West st.   T N 90

Pettipher T. K. & Son, grocers, 14 West st.   T N 11

Priestland Clara (Mrs.), tobccnst. 4 Middle row

Pulker Chas. Seaward, boot repr. 19 Horsefair

Putman Frederick H. waterproof sheet & tent manufacturer, cycle agent, sports & rope dealer ; **tents for hire**, 20 High street

Quiet Woman P.H. (Geo. Pratley), Southcombe

Red Lion P.H. (Arth. Jn. Fry), 8 Albion st

Rice Geo. E. beer retlr. 21 West end

Robertson James Fenwick M.R.C.S.Eng., L.R.C.P. Lond. physician & surgeon, & medical officer to the Institution, 15 Market pl.   T N 6

Rogers Geo. Wltr. tobccnst. 9 New st

Rose Thos. Fredk. dairy farmer, Fowlers Barn farm, London rd

Rowell R. & Sons (Engineers) Ltd. 7 High st.   T N 12

Royal Society for the Prevention of Cruelty to Animals (Mrs. Grace Packer, sec.), 28 High st

Civic Life and Events

Photographed outside the Church Army premises c1940 this civil defence group includes: Left to right, top row: Alf Grantham, Howard Benfield, Frank Jarvis, Des Parsons, ?, Mr Hill (in civies). Second row: Mr Hoare, third from right Jack Brain and at the end Mr Cox. Third row: ?, ?, ?, ? Morris, J. Stapleton, Front row: ?, Mr Watts, Mr Perry, 'Gaffer' Smith (Mayor and Headteacher of the Church of England School).

A bonfire built to celebrate the coronation of King George V.

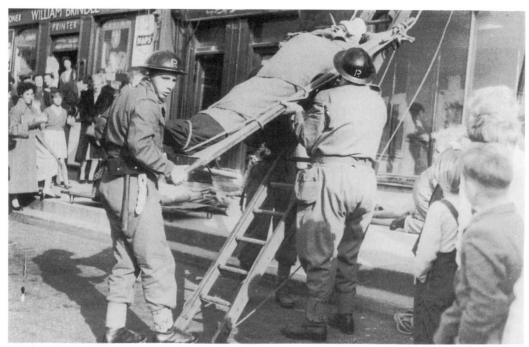

Chipping Norton Home Guard practising a rescue at G.H. Hannis's shop at 10 High Street. As can be seen from this photograph the ladder was not steep enough; by the time the third man was on the ladder the strain was too much and the ladder broke.

Chipping Norton Home Guard. Left to right, middle row: First on right is Mr Benfield. Back row: ?, ?, Pete Grant, Jack Parsons, ?, Jack Candy, 'Cod' Robinson.

Civic Defence 1957. The group includes Brian Powers, Jim Powers, David Clark and Norman Smart.

The Civil defence central room which was possibly in the Oddfellows Hall c1942. Left to right: Margaret Shepherd, Mr King, Jean Smart, Mrs King.

Chipping Norton Town Council during the war. Left to right, front row: Daniel Rutter Simms, Mr Hill, Mr Townley, Mr Warmington, Edgar Smith, ?, Jack Marshall, Bob Major. Middle row: Mr Cuthbert, ?, Mr Swan, Mr Hannis, Mr Craft, George Hannis, Mr Sinden, Mr Jeffries, Back row: ?, Mr Farrant, ?, ?, ?, ?.

Chipping Norton Town Council 1952. Left to right: ?, Mrs King (Deputy Mayor), Miss Webb (Mayor), Jack Marshall, Bob Major, George Warmington, George Hannis. Second row: Harold Lord, ?. Wilf Bursen, ?, George Hughes. Back row: Margery Willets, Mr Whettam, John Chamberlayne, Mr Wykes, Mr Jeffries, ?, Dick Gibbs, Harold Cyphus, Charlie Withers.

Frank Morris, the Town Clerk who left in 1940. For a while Chipping Norton had a part-time Town Clerk appointed by the Borough solicitor, S.G. Farrant of Farrant and Sinden. By c1946/47 the Town Clerk was again full time when Mr K. Holmes was appointed. In 1950 Eric Hood was employed to look after the rates and other financial matters. In 1974 the town lost its Borough Status under the Local Government Act. At this time the staff included the Town Clerk Eugene 'Frank' Cunningham, Eric Hood (Finance Officer), Peter Kennedy, Brian Parsons, Alice Brain, Nigel Leake, John Mitchell (Clerk of the Works), David Hayward, Jean Smart, Jen Tunnicliffe, Ben Lyon (Housing Officer) and Roy Watson (plumber).

H.M. Queen Elizabeth II visiting Chipping Norton 8 April, 1959. In this photograph Mayor Stanley Wykes is introducing Mrs Wykes, Mrs King, Bob Major and George Hannis.

Chipping Norton auxiliary firemen c1945. Left to right, back row: Wilf Bursen, Roy Burford, Cod Robinson, Edgar Morris, Ernie Morris. First row: ? Clacy, Les Slade, ? Waring, ? Robinson, Des Walman, ?, ?, Cyril Withers. Second row: Hilda Prior, ?, George Heritage, ?, Ted Simms, Harry Kite, George

Harrison, Pam Heritage. Front row: Muriel Lines, ?, June Baker, ?, ?, Joyce Jones. (Alan Brain)

Chipping Norton Auxiliary firemen in the 1950s. Left to right, back row: Alan Goodway, Jim Jackson, Trevor Evans, Dave Allen, Michael Hawtin. Front row: George Harrison, Laurie Burden, Horace Woodward, Malcolm Fidler. (Alan Brain)

Opening of the new fire station in the Burford Road, 1969.

Photographed in the British Legion club in the mid 1950s. Left to right: Laurie Burden, Jim Irons, Les 'Dasher' Reeves and Cyril Masters.

It is not certain what these British Legion members won their cups for; the date as shown on the Daily Draw is 1959. Those pictured are left to right: ?, Cyril Masters, Johnny Beck, Mr Wykes, Ray Swan, Jock ?, Jim Irons.

Cyril Masters, Billy Hutchinson and Robert Branch, the standard bearer, in the British Legion after the war, possibly on their way to the Festival of Remembrance in the Albert Hall.

Fire at the Town Hall, 3 March 1950. This photograph was taken by Reg Johnston. After the fire, which was caused by an electrical fault, was extinguished, the mayor's wooden chair which survived the blaze, was placed outside on the top of the steps: it is not known what became of this chair.

Town Hall Fire (Alan Brain). The original Town Hall was erected by public subscription in 1842.

The interior of the Town Hall after the fire.

Spectators at the fire at Hitchmans brewery, 29 June 1922.

The fire at The Quiet Woman public house, 19 April 1967, resulted in the complete destruction of the building in one hour. In this photograph gas cannisters are exploding; some fell only feet away from the firemen. The flames on the first floor give the impression that there is a face at the right-hand window. (R. Stares).

LODGE TERRACE
1 Fisher, Alfred
2 Parsons, James E.
3 Hawtin, Horace D.
4 Rawlings, Elsie
5 Townsend, Albert P.
6 Luckett, Bernard J.
7 Rimell, Charles A.
8 Sanders, Derrick J.
9 Kyte, Albert G.
10 Vinall, Thomas H.

LONDON ROAD
Hartwell, G. R. Ltd., motor & agricultural engineers. Tel. 41 & 366
Major & Major, motor engineers
Cato, Frank, Police Station
Twaites, Janet R., Ash Tree Cottage
1 Sherburn, Brian S.
1 Slack, Walter
3 Morris, John H.
4 Baker, Arthur E.
5 Moulder, Jim A.
6 Preston, Charles
6a Gulliver, Ernest E. G.
7 Major, Robert A. H.
8 Coles, Ann E.
9 Keen, Donald W.
Gibbs, Francis J., Alvestone
Simms, Alfred W., The Limes
10 Balfour, Ruth E.
11 Aries, George A.
12 Wright, James
13 Stanbridge, Bernard
14 Stanbridge, Lawrence
15 Keen, Lilian G.
Wagon and Horses, The
17 Morris, Leonard
18 Gough, Charles A.
19 Benfield, Joseph W. T.
20 Button, Samuel G.
21 Halford, George
22 Salmon, Mary E.
23 Campin, James
24 St. Joseph's Convent
25 Digwood, Henry M., Rock Hill Farm
Kilgallon, Rev. Edward, Holy Trinity Rectory
26 Cotshill Hospital
Rose, Thomas F., Fowlers Barn Farm
Pollard, Kenneth B., New Chalford Farm
Rose, Douglas R., Corwen

MARKET PLACE
Heron, S. R., draper, Manchester House
Styles, James, & Whitlock, auctioneers & estate agents. Tel. 39
6 **Craft Walter & Sons Ltd., agricultural, corn & seed merchants. Tel. 215-216**
10 Stockton Sons & Fortescue, solicitors. Tel. 40

10 Thornton & Thornton, accountants. Tel. 40
Bignell, H., Corner Café, baker
Webb, A. A. & Son, drapers & house furnishers. Tel. 71
Unicorn, The, hotel. Tel. 318
15 Latcham, Dr. Peter R.
16a National Provincial Bank Ltd.
16a Coombes, R. H. & Co. accountants
16a Sharpe, Stanley J.
17 International Stores, grocers
17 Slade, Leslie, H. E.
18 Midland Bank Ltd.
20 Freeborn, George A., butcher
21 Benfield, J. W.
Fox Hotel, The. Tel. 158
Taylor, George H., Old Bank House

MARKET STREET
1 Sole, F., butcher
2 Dix, Thomas
3 Tyler, A., greengrocer
4 Robertson, M. M., antique dealer
5 Lewis, F., builder
6 Foster, Alfred
7 Warrick, George E. H.
7 **Burbidge & Sons (Chipping Norton) Ltd., builders. Tel. 70**
9 Jarvis, James V.
10 Wilson, William C.
11 Duncombe, George H., grocer
12 Spelling, Reginald S.

MIDDLE ROW
Bunch of Grapes, The, inn
Curtis, K., draper
4 Phoenix Cafe & Restaurant
5 Eastmans, dry cleaners
6 Bennett, E. R., grocer
7 Berry, J.
8 Freeman, Bert, hairdresser
9 Hibling & Buckingham, ophthalmic opticians
9 Preece, A. T. & R., grocers
10 Phelps, Stanley P.
Burbidge, confectioner
17 Dodson, Ada M.
19 Oxford Mail & Times
20 Burden, Louise
21 Griffin, Bertram J.
Dairy Shop, The
Parrot, The, inn

NEW STREET
Blue Lion, The
7 Sims, J. G., fishmonger
9 Hill, Arthur J.
11 Brain, John F.
13 Gunston, Raymond F.
15 Pratley, Eric
17 Margetts, Alec

19 Scarsbrook, Frederick W.
21 Preece, George S.
23 Batts, Alfred
Austin, Ernest H., Hill Lawn Cottage
25 Robinson, George H.
27 Bridgewater, Reginald C.
29 Sandles, George
31 Caswell, Sidney C.
33 Gibbs, Annie
35 Webb, Sybil A.
37 Burbidge, Leslie
39 Leech, Percival J.
51 Sadler, Florence
53 Guy, Ida
55 Hall, Thomas J.
57 Richardson, Gertrude E.
59 Flick, Peter
65 Meades, Emily M.
67 Padley, Ernest
Ward, John S., Ivycroft
4 Hovard, Frederick A.
8 White, Henry R.
10 Langton, H.
12 Lewis, Joseph
14 Lewis, Michael
16 Hearn, Edgar J.
18 Morris, Edith S. M.
20 Bedwin, Eric T.
26 Lovering, Gwyn W. J.
32 Wright, Anne A.
34 Jeffries, William C.
36 Simms, John E.
38 Griffiths, Rhys
40 Gunston, Frederick H.
42 Wiggins, Hilda
44 Margetts, Percival E.
46 Packer, Hubert H.
48 Buck, Harold
50 Sutcliffe, James C.

Dunstan House
Chaplin, Ronald
Mitchell, James T. G.
Jones, Evelyn
Watts, Cyril E. N.
Willey, Lydia
Clifton, Cyril T. E.
56 McDonald, Walter
58 Longshaw, John C.
60 Perry, John A.
62 Lewis, Ada
64 Jocham, Louisa
70 Duley, Eric
70 Dyson, Hubert
McDowall, Howard, The Old Mill
National Children's Home Penshurst

OLDNER
Adshead, Philip, Oldner House
Terry, Christobel, Oldner House Farm
Lloyd, Frank, Oldner House Farm Cottage
Salter, Ernest R., 1 Oldner Bungalow
Walton, Leslie, 2. Oldner Bungalow

OVER NORTON ROAD
War Memorial Hospital
Nurses' Home, Chestnuts

Barber, William A., Masonic Lodge
Francis, Harry, The Aviary
Sinden, Thomas S., Braewaithe
Jones, Basil J., Clevecot
Burden, George R., Watcombe
Elliott, Rupert R., Blue Haze
Graham, George G., Selsdon
Price, Francis D., Shere
Morris, William P., Brantwood
Comer, Percy R., Pentire
Davis, Douglas C., Willowfold
Hewett, George F., Eversley
Rowbotham, Jack, Bryn Lea
Acton, Cecil R., Pyrton
White, Elsie M., Holmlea
Smith, Thomas F., Ellendale
Hughes, Ernest, Cot View
Hebborn, Arthur E., Fairhaven
Gerrard, Geoffrey F., The Close
Peddle, George S. R., Rozelle
Robinson, Ernest H., D.S.O., M.C., M.A.
Brown, Reginald G. H., Wendover
Pratt, Alfred A., Hillside
Whettam, William J., Silverdale

PARADISE TERRACE
1 Edwards, Bessie
2 May, William R.
3 Quartermain, John A.
4 Hannis, Josephine M. T.
5 Herbert, Rosslyn L.
6 Smith, Marian H.
7 Spencer, Daisy F.
8 Fry, Albert E.

PEMBRIDGE TERRACE
1 Roberts, William J.
2 Ward, Ronald
3 Kennedy, William E.
4 Keen, George A.
5 Beesley, Harry C.

PORTLAND PLACE
1 Darnborough, Mabel
3 Brown, Harry
4 Woodward, William
5 Simms, Sarah E.
6 Ackerman, Albert H.
7 Kail, Winifred E.
8 Lainchbury, Mansell W.
9 Webb, Frank H.
10 Harwood, Dorothy B.

ROCK HILL
Stopford, General Sir Montagu, Rock Hill House

Recreation

This dance took place in a room at the back of the Temperance Hotel in the early 1900s. One of the ladies is Mrs Padley, but unfortunately it has not been recorded which one she is.

The date on the back of this photograph is 5 July 1917 which presumably is the date of this Baby Show. The babies appear to encompass a wide age range and to our eyes the layers of clothes are singularly inappropriate for a summer's day.

Photographed on a truck belonging to the Volunteer Fire Brigade in Middle Row, left to right: C. Jeffries, Ernest Barlow, H. Barlow, ?, E. or B. Simms.

Chipping Norton Flower Show in the early 1910s.

CHIPPING NORTON MORRIS DANCERS
HOSPITAL SATURDAY 1910. 9

Looking along West Street on Hospital Saturday in 1910, Johnston's the saddlers on the right. The caption says Chipping Norton Morris Dancers, but it looks as if schoolchildren are taking a large part in the display. On the right is Fred 'Father' Lewis, also known as 'Conk' Lewis, a local builder and undertaker and a notable character in Chipping Norton. He started the Scout troop in Chipping Norton, supposedly before Baden Powell had his camp at Brownsea Island. He also brought baseball to England and, as can be imagined, Chipping Norton was for some years the national baseball champions.

The Chipping Norton Co-Operative Women's Guild in the late 1920s. The group includes Mrs Marshall, Evelyn Herbert and Mrs Brassington.

The Church Army photographed on 11 February 1923. Front row: 'Perk' Dixon (with a moustache) is next to the officer. Middle row: ?, – Brain, Harold Wright, Cecil Watts, ?, ?, ?, ?, Alfred Grantham, ?, ?. The first few houses in Dunstan Avenue were faced with stones salvaged from the demolition of the Church Army Hall.

The Committee of the Fur and Feather Club in 1939. Left to right, back row: Billy Grantham, Cyril Clifton, Raymond Simms, John Hannis, Dennis Hovard. Middle row: George Stowe, Gilbert Giles, Rhoda Burford, Mrs Young, Mrs Burford, Mrs Britain. Front row: Fred Hewitt, Paul Crossfield, Mrs Crossfield, Jack Simms, ?. One of the best known shops in Chipping Norton was Langtons owned by 'Poppy' Langton. Inside there were a couple of forms to sit on while you had an ice cream or a drink. At the back of the shop was a small room used for meetings and it was here that the Fur and Feather Club used to meet showing rabbits and pigeons and such. The club used to have shows around the area such as at the Manor House, the grounds of Dr O'Shea's surgery and also in a marquee in London Road on the football ground. Paul Crossfield was the local vet who had premises in Albion Street.

Hospital Saturday 1908, Webb's department store float. Left to right: Mr and Mrs Mann (he was Webb's manager), Beatrice Hannis, ?, ?, ?, ?, ?, Harry Hinton (horseman in bowler hat). Mr and Mrs Mann look as if they have been added to the photograph at a later date.

Hartwell and Barlow's truck on Hospital Saturday in the 1920s. The driver is Ernie Hughes who worked for Hitchmans.

Hospital Saturday, 1933 photographed on Castle Banks, where rubbish was tipped. The crowd watched Reg Johnston entertain. Included in this group are: Ken Benfield, Mrs Perry, Reg Shepard, Jim Shepard and Bert Tanner. Hospital Saturday was held annually on the last Saturday in July to raise money for the local hospital and was an anticipated event.

The Kazoo Band c1933 on the Town Hall steps. The group includes: George Walton, John Hannis, Cyril Warmington, John Aldridge, Mr J.W. Freeman in charge (a barber), Henry Wilson, Laurence Abbott, Raymond Simms, Gerald Walman, Mavis Lord, Norma Tollet, Greta Abbott, Joan Pratt, Joan Berry, Norma Lines.

Left to right, back row: W. Kirby, C. Smart, L. Smart, J. Thornton, J. Powers, J. Candy. Front row: P. Perry, B. Reddington, P. Heritage, J. Tanner, D. Murphy, E. Kirby, P. Herbert. The leader is Mr Perry.

Chipping Norton Silver Band

In March 1935 Harry Pickett formed Chipping Norton Silver Band with Jim, Les and Alf Pickett, Peter Morris, Reg Benfield, Bertie Buggins, Vic Harris and Bill Tanner who had all resigned from the Salvation Army at the same time. Although Harry was almost 21, the average age of the others was 14–15. Despite a lack of musical knowledge and with no money and only two old cornets between them, it was decided to meet in Mrs Pickett's front room with a view to forming a band. Contact with a musical instrument repairer in Northampton, Fred Tompkins & Son, for advice resulted in the firm loaning the burgeoning band all that was needed to play, including a bass and side drum for 28 days. After this time, if the band was not successful the instruments would be reclaimed; if successful a down payment of £10 plus £4 monthly payments were to be made.

The band's original name was the Chipping Norton Junior Temperance Band, and all new members were to be under 21. Harry Pickett was appointed Bandmaster, Chairman and Acting Secretary, Jim Pickett was Deputy Bandmaster and Reg Benfield's grandfather was Treasurer; they all remained in these posts until 1940. The band members all resolved to be teetotal.

The band immediately started to play in the town and surrounding villages with the Treasurer and May Kitchen collecting money. By 29 April, £10 2s was paid into the Midland Bank and the £10 payment was made to F. Tomkins & Sons. Rehearsals were almost nightly and many engagements were undertaken; in June a cornet and tenor horn were purchased for £1.10s and £1 17s 6d, respectively. New members came forward and, as the Old Primitive Methodist Chapel was empty, the Trustees suggested that in return for its free use the band could play the hymns at their Camp Meetings. This was readily agreed to and rehearsals were held there until 1940. In August Mr Tompkins received his remaining money three months ahead of time. About 1937 a small percentage was paid to the players as some recompense for their efforts. In July 1937 the band played for the Church Army Fete and received £1; this was where the first real band photograph was taken. By the second anniversary the band had purchased uniforms from the Uniform Equipment Co. of London; the bill read: deposit £25. Balance £63 11s 6d for 20 complete uniforms and 1 Bandmaster outfit.

By May 1940, 20 of the 22 members had been called up; all but one returned. Vic Harris, euphonium player, died of wounds and smallpox in hospital in Alexandria. The band has gone from strength to strength since then. Various competitions have been entered over the years, many successfully, and it is a credit to the founders that 65 years on the band still flourishes.

Chipping Norton Town Band photographed probably just after the end of World War I. C.W. Hannis is the conductor and other band members include Lionel Smith, Fred Baker and the Margett brothers.

The Chipping Norton band photographed in the early 1930s. The metal drinking fountain on the left had four metal cups attached to it by chains; tramps used to get water here. The fountain was removed during World War II. On the right are the premises of The Unicorn Hotel which were demolished in the 1970s.

Photographed at the Silver Band Fete in the late 1940s. Pictured here are left to right: Bob Arnold (who played Tom Forrest in the Archers), Mrs Slade, Harry Pickett, Mrs Johnstone and Mr Johnston. Unfortunately the Union Jack is upside down!

Members of Chipping Norton Silver Band, winners of a quartet competition c1952. Left to right, back row: 'Nobby' Chalice, Harry Pickett. Front row: Fred Hunt, Howard McDowell, Reg Benfield, Norman Dix.

Chipping Norton Silver Band c1952/53. Left to right, front row: Chris Thornton, Laurie Burden, Lionel Smith, Harry Pickett, Norman Dix, John Hannis, Peter Morris. Middle row: Reg Benfield, Cecil Smith, Kathy Smith, Peter Dix, Michael Oliver, Norman Pickett, Chris Heath, Jim Hall, Jim Pickett. Back row: Fred Heath, Bill Tanner, Oscar Smith, Fred Hunt, Howard McDowell, Frank Acock, Vic Pickett, Austin Smith, ? (drummer; kept flute shop), Keith Pickett, Leo Helmore, Ted Burden, Ray Burden.

The Band at Remembrance Sunday in 1950. Left to right, front row: Michael Oliver, Jim Pickett, Jim Hall, Billy Tanner, Phil Knight. Second row: Kathy Smith, Lionel Smith, Oscar Smith, Chris Thornton, John Hannis. Third row: Keith Pickett, Aubrey Aldridge, Laurie Burden, Norman Dix. Reggie Benfield and Johnnie Fudge are stood on their own. Back row; Leo Helmore, Fred Burden, Austin Smith, Ray Burden, Vic Pickett, Fred Hunt, Albie Burden, Howard McDowell.

A school play at the Town Hall c1930. Left to right, back row: Bill Harris, Tony Padley, Ronald Ship, Eva Naylor, Jim Shepard, Henry Tidmarsh, ?, Roy Withers, Jean Hannis, Sybil Calcutt, — Smart, ?. Front row: Les Sewell, ?, — Trinder, Jim Pick. Although the title of the play has not been recalled it was something to do with the King being ill; Jim Shepard was the doctor.

Chipping Norton dramatic society in the production *Pink String and Sealing Wax* c1949. Left to right, back row: Ann Castell, ?. Front row: Mavis Cross, Harold Coram, Mrs Briggs, Rachel Hainey.

Teddy Dix Band in the 1950s. Left to right: Les Picket, Joe Townley, Jack Clapton, Ken Padley, Bert Ackerman and Teddy Dix. (Alan Brain)

The Norton Hall, formerly the Oddfellow's Hall, was a popular venue for young people in the days of rock and roll. Teddy Dix and his band, later the Blue Tones, often played here. The Norton Hall was called the old cinema, the new cinema being built in New Street c1935/36.

Photographed at a dance at the Town Hall in the 1950s. Left to right: Gilbert Berry, Mrs Berry, Percy Goodwin. (Alan Brain).

The Regent Cinema. During World War II the buildings on the right were taken over by the Americans and used for accommodation. After 1945 they were renovated.

The interior of the Regent Cinema.

Right, from left to right: Graham Embra, Geoff Potter, Les Leach. Mr Leach did several jobs, helping with the gardens, painting the stones at the side of the road, clearing up as well as helping show the films. On Saturday evenings the cinema was usually filled to its capacity, 500 seats. The cinema had its own car park. Wednesday and Saturday evenings and some Sundays were also very busy times; sometimes people stood. Records were played during the intervals and royalties were paid for their use, the staff used to put the records they liked on more often to earn extra royalties for their favourite artists. Sometimes the heating was raised intentionally to try and sell more ice-creams although this was probably counter productive with the higher cost of the heating off setting the increased ice-cream takings. Sometimes the posters were deliberately changed to attract the audience's attention, for example Jewel in the Sun might be changed to Fuel in the Sun. Films came on several reels and it was necessary to put them on at the right time. Once during the "Valley of Decision", with Greer Garson, the operatives were wrestling on the floor and, realising a new reel was required, hurriedly put one on, but unfortunately it was Donald Duck.

Mr and Mrs Harry Baker with their two sons John and Roger c1946/47 when Mr Baker was employed by the cinema.

Chipping Norton Women's Institute Christmas party in the Town Hall, 1953.

Those identified are: 1. Minnie Birtinshaw, 2 Maureen Coram, 3. Joan Baldwin, 4. Mrs Caroline Gardner, 5. Mrs Williams, 6. Mrs Cecily Hunt, 7. Mrs Watkins, 8. ? Gibbs, 9. Mrs Roache, 10. Mrs Luckett, 11. Mrs Miles, 12. Mrs Roberts, 13. Mrs Mealin, 14. Mrs Stobart, 15. Mrs Mitchell, 16. Mrs Simms, 17. Joan White, 18. Mrs Beard, 19. Mrs Townsend, 20. Mrs Gibbard, 21. Mrs Davis, 22. Mrs Lily Thompson, 23. Eileen Forbes, 24. Mrs Kenyon, 25. Mrs Sandles, 26. Mrs Powers, 27. Mrs Heritage, 28. Mrs Aggie Harwood, 29. Mrs Tipping, 30. Mrs Howes, 31. Mrs Franklin, 32. Mrs Hawtin, 33. Mrs Sheffield, 34. Mrs Dorothy Lewis, 35. Mrs Eileen Betteridge, 36. Mrs Stockley, 37. Mrs Coram, 38. Miss Joynes, 39. Mrs Stella Burden, 40. Nancy Horwood, 41. Mrs McDowell, 42. Connie ? 43. Mrs Everilde Davis, 44. Mrs Dealey, 45. Mrs Fiddler, 46. Mrs Helmore, 47. Mrs Nancy Hall, 48. Ethel Burbidge, 49. Mrs Stanbridge, 50. Mrs Stevens, 51. Peggy White, 52. Mrs Walman, 53. Mrs Alec Hawtin, 54. Mrs Kitchen. Also in this group are Mrs Morse, Mrs M. Robinson, Maureen Ball, Edna Fry, Mrs B. Cox, Miss Hapgood and Mrs Shadbolt.

The Ladies Baseball team c1930. Left to right, front row: Nancy Hieatt, ? Hands, ? Pratt, ? Hardy, ? Shepard, ? Shepard (sisters), Hilda Pratt, ? Walman, Evelyn Hawtin, Stella Gardner. Middle row: Alec Hawtin, Olive Gardner, Sybil Calcut, Zyllpha Tanner, Doll Lowe, ? Powell, ? Dixon, ? Webb, Mrs Gardner, ? Birtinshaw, Beattie Birtinshaw. Back row: Dick Harding, ?, Fortescue Sewell, ?, ?, Mr Lewis, ?, ?, ?. The captains of these two ladies' teams were Olive Gardner and Doll Lowe.

Chipping Norton Keep Fit Club c1952. Left to right, back row: Joan Burden, ?, Barbara Carter, Dorothy Burden, ?, Anna Watkins, Mabel Perry, Joy Newman, Susan Austin,?, Anne Coltman, ?, ?. Second row: Susan Kitchen, Daphne Williams, Wendy Simmonds, ? Walman, Kathleen Preecen, ?, ?, Janet Tiping, Ann Priestland, Maureen Stanley, Ann Peachey, Elaine Tarrant. Third row: Judith Walman, Avis Rowbotham, Pat Gibbard, Linda Walman, Christine Howling, ?, ?, Pamela Benfield, Freda Webb, Ceilia Austin, Muriel White, Sonia Hitchcock, Gillian Jones, Lesley Slade. Fourth row: Valerie Davies, Beatrice McKnight, ?, Joan Marshall, ?, ?, ?, ?, Marilyn Grantham, ? Clacy, ?, Elizabeth Hunt, ?. Fifth row: Stella McDowell, Pat Sale, ?, Celia Parry, ?, Carol Hitchcock, Judith Clacy, ?, ?, Denise Roche, Janet Heald. Front row: Adrienne Chaplin, Georgina Thornton, Sonia Simmonds, Sue Hood, Elizabeth Elliott, ?, Ann ?, ?, Judith Franklin, ? Haney, ?, ?, Julie Burden, ?.

The Pearl Assurance Company Staff Dinner, 17 February 1949. Standing left to right, back row: Peter Flick, Frances Flick, ?, ?, Mrs Barker (kept the Kings Arms), Barbara Masters, ?, Jack Smart, Connie Smart, ?, ?, ?, ?, ?, ?, ?, ?, ?, Everilde Davis' mother, ?. Seated: Walter Elliot, Mrs Pemmie Masters, Mr Owen, Mrs Elliot, Cyril Masters, Mr Harris. On the left-hand side of the table: ?, ?, Mr and Mrs West, ?, Eric ?, ?. On the right-hand side of the table: ?, Arch Steel, Mrs Steel, ?, ?, Everilde Davis, Joe Davis. The photograph was probably taken in the White Hart Hotel. The company held dinners every so often when senior management came to assess how the firm was doing at a local level.

Photographed at a Co-op dinner, these employees are left to right: Bill White, Percy Barnes, Mrs Barnes and Jim Shepard, probably in the mid-1950s.

Chipping Norton Guides with Mayor Arthur Brindle outside the old Boots and Giles shoe shop in the late 1940s. Pictured with Mr Brindle is Mavis Cross. Mr Brindle kept a stationers and newsagents in High Street.

Chipping Norton Guides off on camp c1967. Seated, left to right: Caroline Putman, Kathleen Muston, ? Harrison, Jane Craft, ? Harrison, Susan Blake, Sheila Graham, ?, ?. Standing, left to right: Mrs Mollie Wykes, ?, ?, ?, Sylvia Rose who has been involved with the Guides for many years.

Valentine's Day, 1953. The boy on the right is Adrian 'Joe' Bridges. (Alan Brain)

On Valentine's Day, 14 February, children would gather in the Market Place before school and sing outside the shops: 'Please to give us a Valentine, I'll be yours if you'll be mine.' The shopkeepers threw their wares to the children: the International Stores threw heated pennies from a shovel which the children quickly dropped into cans of water attached to their belts and Rocky Leach often threw sweets from a Quality Street tin which were quickly snapped up whilst Miss Bird also threw sweets. The Temperance Hotel premises at 9 High Street were successively occupied by Alfred Bird and his daughter who kept the premises to sell toys and confectionery as well as running a restaurant and boarding house. Miss Bird's shop 'was a joy to small children; the counter was crowded, the shelves were laden. Everything was there and everything was cheap and within the range of a child's pocket money. Miss Bird was well known to commercial travellers who appreciated her kindness, her good cooking and the extreme cleanliness of her rooms.' By 1948 these premises were occupied by the Co-op.

Scout group c1950/51. Left to right, front row: ?, ? Branson, John Grantham, Peter Dix, Martin Harris, Terry Cox, Tony Pick, ? Stevens. Middle row: Bobby Pick, ?, Ernie Sandles, Ron Stares, Graham Miles, Michael Hawtin. Back row: ? Webb, ? Taylor, ? Burden, ?, John Caswell, ? Haney, Norman Miles.

Before World War II there was a Boy's Brigade attached to the Methodist Church but this ceased when the minister left. When his replacement, Ronald Frost, arrived Ron Stares asked him if he would restart the Brigade. As Mr Frost only had experience of scouting it was decided to start the 6th Chipping Norton scouts. Before the war Ron Stares was a troop leader but on his return from the war he was appointed as scout leader.

Coronation tea party at Spring Street, 1953, inside the Salvation Army hall. Included in this group are: Mary Scarsbrook, Johnnie Scarsbrook, Colonel John Chamberlayne (Mayor), Mrs Daphne Chamberlayne, Mrs Rhoda Burford, Wendy Burford, John Burford, Mrs Walman, Mrs Bird, Albert Woodward, Rose Woodward, Mrs Hancock, Geraldine Walman, Mrs Gibbs, Nancy Shadbolt and baby, Kath Timms and baby and Cis Parsons.

Coronation Tea at the Leys 1953 inside one of Craft's sheds. Seated on the right: ? Haynes, ?, ? Cooper, ? Edwards, Alan Watkins, Paul Bennett, Pat Bennett, Jean Coltman. Seated on the left the tall boy is ? Cooper. Also included are Keith and John Hainsworth. The adults in this group include: Mrs Haynes and Eileen Forbes and baby, Mrs Hughes, Mr Killeby and Mrs Joaquim.

Chipping Norton Co-operative Society coalmen tug of war team in the early 1950s. The team are left to right: Jack Roper, Bob Waring, Charlie Harwood, Walter Pickett, Bill Yates, Laurie Burden, Fred Thresher and Fred Watson. The gentleman on the left in the raincoat is Bill Ward.

Looking down New Street, c1956/57. The cyclists are probably part of the Milk Race. Both sides of the street display the sign 'Waiting Pedestrians'; as there are no vehicles in sight it is likely that traffic has been stopped for the race to pass through the town. John Betteridge is standing on the far right.

Photographed at Finsbury Place during the war. Left to right: Mr and Mrs Dyer, Mrs Margetts, Mr Margetts and Mrs Margetts snr. Unfortunately it has not proved possible to identify the children. (A. Brain)

A schoolgirls' outing in the 1950s taken at Hill Lawn Court; the building in the background is Finsbury Place. This group includes Laura Coram , ? Rogers, Ann and Elspeth McDowell, Jennifer Smith, ? Simmons and Miss Dixon.

Photographed during the building of the football pavilion, Darkie Hawtin, Cyril Masters, Arthur Carpenter, ?, Frank Hawtin.

The supporters club was opened by G.H. Hannis on November 7 1953.

In the 1890s Chipping Norton played St Barnabas from Oxford. Following a draw there was a replay at Charlbury. The referee supplied by the Oxford team did not meet with the Chipping Norton team's approval; after the match (which they presumably lost) they tried to throw the referee into the stream. A resulting inquiry by the County Association resulted in Chipping Norton being suspended but this was presumably not too problematic as they formed their own league.

Chipping Norton Swifts 1954?5. Left to right, back row: Fred Panting, Ray Simms, Derek Smith, Pat Hancock, John Hicks, John Roberts, Edwin Simms, Barney Mulhearn, Mr Heritage. Front row: ?, Cyril Smart, Brian Pinfold and ? Tilly.

Chipping Norton Town Football Club 1974. Left to right, back row: Mick Kennard (team manager), Clive Baker, Eamon Kearns, Trevor Davis, John Rose, Dave Munslow, Ian Richardson, Phil Lines. Front row: Derek Souch, Alan Hellyer, Peter Hutchinson, Steve Slaughter and Gino Crognale.

Although these boys played for Salford U14s, they were mostly 'Chippy' lads. Left to right, back row: Michael Hannis, Michael Smart, Martin Clifton. Front row: Johnny Guy, ? Hemmings and Stuart Watts. This photograph was taken at a competition at Charlbury. (R. Stares)

Opening of the Chipping Norton Cricket Club. Left to right, back row: Horace Woodward, Mrs Bob Harding, Tom Moulder, Bob Harding, Billy Hawtin, Horace Hawtin, Albert Woodward. Front row: Arthur Carpenter, Gilbert Berry (manager of Webbs), Cyril Masters, Cyril Allen, Fred Pinfold.

The Opening of the Chipping Norton Cricket Pavilion by the Mayor, Councilor Brindle, 7 May 1950. The group includes: Harry White, Mr Perry, Mr Reason, Brian Evans, Mansell Lainchbury, John Hannis, Mr Gibbs, Councilor and Mrs Brindle, Mrs Perry, Ada Lainchbury, Norman Boulter, Joe Davis and Jean Addicot.

The cricket tea ladies. Left to right back row: Mrs Everilde Davies, Connie Reeves, Mrs Sole, Jean Hannis,?, Ada Lainchbury. Front row: Mrs Franklin, ?, Mrs Mitchell, ?, Mrs Roughton.

To celebrate the Festival of Britain in 1951, a football match was played with both teams in fancy dress. The captain of Master's Marauding Mudlarks was Cyril Masters and the captain of Worth's Worthless Wanderers was Mr Worth of Worth's buses. This photograph includes: Horace Woodward, 'Knocker' White (who kept the fish and chip shop) and, of course, the two captains.

The match was held on the common and by the time this photograph was taken during the match the costumes appear to have mainly disappeared except for Mr Masters who, by chance, has managed to retain his top hat.

Some of the participants in fancy dress.

Outside the Red Lion. Left to right, front row: Bill Yates senior, Stan Phelps. Middle row: P. Reason, Fred Pick, Boxer Griffin. Back row: Bill Yates, Dick Hicks, Butch Withers.

Outside the Red Lion. Left to right: Bill Yates senior, his son also Bill Yates, Graham Page and John Page.

The two houses in the centre of this photograph were demolished to make access from High Street to Albion Street; this part was known locally as Hell Fire Corner. Between these two houses was a passageway which led through to Pig Yard: the garden of the Red Lion used to run down towards the Fox Hotel and its right-hand wall was once the back of at least seven pig sties, hence the name. There were originally nine cottages on the left-hand side but these were demolished due to their slum-like conditions.

Inside the Red Lion pub in the early 1960s. Left to right, back row: Horace 'Darky Hawtin', Jock Hutchinson, Dot Brown, Albert Hawtin. Front row; Fred Perry, Jack Smart, Cyril Smart, and Keith Tiffin.

Inside The Blue Lion at 6 New Street in the 1950s, it closed in 1969. Left to right: ?, John Knight, ?, Laurie Annis (the landlord), Fred Chapman, Fred Timms, Tom Widdows. (Alan Brain)

Men's darts team in the 1950s. This group includes Mr Perry, Alf Smith, Mr Watson, Harry Kite, Vic Cooper, Mr Harris, Bert Somerton and Wally Pickett. (Alan Brain)

Ladies' darts team in the 1950s. This group includes: ? Smart, Dot Freeman, Mrs Harding, Ada Smart, Mrs Stokes, Doll Brown, Mrs Boobeer (who came from Cornwall) and Iris Brain. (Alan Brain)

The old Liberal Club and Bates' shop on the corner of the Burford Road

Photographed inside the Liberal Club. Left to right: Bill Jakeman, Roy Woodward, Edgar Johnstone, Harry Hovard, ? (manager of Hilton's shoe shop), ?, Alf Carter. (A. Brain).

Chipping Norton Carnival trolley races in 1965 photographed on the recreation ground in Worcester Road. This group includes Keith Millard, Colin Hovard, Michael Hannis, Rebecca Hohnbaum, Tony and David Stares. (R. Stares)

This photograph of the Holy Trinity Church summer fete was taken about 1967. The pony and trap belonged to Mr and Mrs Sherbourne of Lyneham near Kingham and on board are Maureen Hannis, John Ford and Debra Harding. (R. Stares)

This Royal Mail coach, which covered the London to Worcester run, visited Trust House Forte Hotels to raise money for the Queen's Silver Jubilee in 1977. The Heythrop Hunt staged a fake hold up. Photographed on the coach are Marilyn, Joanne and John Grantham, the Mayor.

Mrs Arnold organised a 'Victorian Event' in aid of the Silver Band. Pictured here are Mrs Arnold, Tom Stroud (Mayor), Ronnie Barker, Harry Pickett and Mrs Gardner and Mrs Edes.

Families and People

The Moulder Band were all members of one family. Left to right, back row: Frank (cornet), Bill (cornet) and Jim (tenor horn). Middle row: Tom (bass), Jack (euphonium) and in the front is Bob (tenor horn).

Elizabeth and Edward Hannis with their children Bessie, Edwin and Minnie at No. 1 Paradise Terrace, Chipping Norton.

The Packer family enjoying a picnic.

Photographed on Good Friday in 1912, Frank Packer's son, Basil, finds a stick (above left) which Frank cuts out (above right) and makes into a walking stick (below).

The Grantham family outside the Toll House at 25 Burford Road c1910. Left to right, back row: Nellie Grantham, James (b. 1860), Grantham, Leah Grantham, Evelyn Grantham. Front row: Alfred Grantham (b. 1904), William Grantham and George Grantham. When he was 14, James Grantham lied about his age to obtain employment and support his family after his father was killed falling off the roof of the Unicorn Public House in Market Place.

The Toll House at 25 Burford Road. In 1839 the tolls taken here amounted to £240; the system was abolished in 1876.

James and Leah Grantham photographed on 30 June 1923.

The Burford Road 28 March 1916 with No. 25 on the left. Photographed here are Evelyn(?) and Leah Grantham, the boy on the snow on the left is Alfred Grantham.

Evelyn (née Grantham) and Harry Herbert inside the Toll House at 25 Burford Road. Harry was a postman.

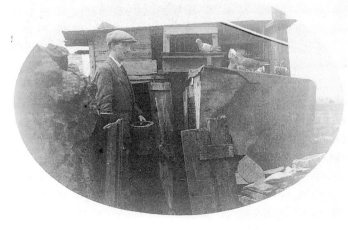

When Bill Guy became homeless, Evelyn and Harry Herbert took him in at No. 25 Burford Road. He lived there in the old bakehouse which was fitted out with a chair and bed. He is photographed here, sometime in the 1940s, with the pigeons he kept.

The wedding of Cyril Smart and Minnie Rose Parsons c1927. Left to right, front row: Frank Smart, Jack Smart, Mrs Smart, Hilda Smart, ?, ?, ?, Ada Smart, Granny Parsons, Grampy Parsons, ?. Middle row: ?, ?, Ag Walman, Bill Smart, Cyril Smart, Minnie Rose Smart (née Parsons), ?, ?, ?. Top row on the left is Frank Smart.

The Burbidge family. Left to right, back row: Gilbert Burbidge, Maggie Burbidge, Les Burbidge, Mrs Carrington (née Burbidge), Percy Burbidge. Front row: Fred Burbidge, Mrs Burbidge, ?.

The Wilkins family photographed c1920 inside The Mount. The Wilkins were a prominent local family; Mr Wilkins was a partner in Wilkins and Toy solicitors, and was also Mayor and Town Councillor.

Burford Terrace in the early years of the twentieth century, now demolished. Some of the people who lived here were Miss Kitchen, Mrs Hunt, Mrs Chapman and Mr and Mrs Kitchen whose daughter May married Harry Pickett.

Percy Simms at the bottom of the 'tower' and his assistant at the top getting ready to take a photograph. The actual event is unknown. The building to the left is Ivy House and to the right the Bunch of Grapes. (Alan Brain)

Left: Jessie and Frederick Tipping by the garage at West End Farm in 1944, with flagon and picnic basket.

Right: Taken c1928 at Meades Farm outside the front room window. Left to right, front row: Fred Tipping, Barbara Honour, Bert Tipping. Middle row: Annie Tipping and Nellie Pauling. At the back is Nancy Pauling. This photograph was taken with a box camera which was acquired by saving coupons from Horniman's tea.

Left: Leonard and Annie Pauling in 1943 photographed in the garden of the 'Dower House', Meades Farm. Mr Pauling sold the farm just after this time for £9,000.

Right: Photographed near the old flour mill on the Churchill Road c1932. This group includes Annie Pauling, Nancy Allen (née Pauling), Sid Allen, Mrs Tipping, Annie Tipping, Bert Tipping, Fred Tipping, Mr and Mrs Weston and Horace Weston. Picnics were regularly held here; the jug contained homemade lemonade.

AUG·13·1938

On 13 August 1938 Harry Pickett married May Kitchen. In this photograph the bride and groom are leaving the church, Harry's fellow band members forming a guard of honour. Harry Pickett was born in Enstone but moved to Chipping Norton at an early age when his father was called up during World War I. Starting as an apprentice at the International Tea Company, Mr Pickett became manager of the Co-op c1955. He learnt to play the cornet but just as he was going to join the Borough band it folded so Mr Pickett joined the Salvation Army Band instead. After some disagreement with the Officers c1935, he left and started Chipping Norton Temperance Band, later Chipping Norton Silver Band.

John Hannis and Lady Hawkyard on the common in the late 1930s.

Looking from the common toward Bliss's Tweed Mill. The cows are, left to right: Dewberry, Rose, Magpie, ?, Bess and Polly!

John and Peter Grantham outside 13 Distons Lane c1950. It is just possible to make out their father, Alfred Grantham, in the window. John had broken his arm when he fell off a swing on the common. Other residents in Distons Lane were:

Fred Baker, the manager of Pettiphers, was the bugler at armistice day and was always practising. He was burnt to death in his house in Distons Lane c1970.

Mrs Hands lived at No. 15 Distons Lane and was also burnt to death in the late 1940s when a candle set light to her bed.

When television was in its infancy only Frank Cox in Distons Lane had a TV. On Saturdays all the neighbouring children would congregate with refreshments in front of the 9-inch Bush set.

Mrs Siggers lived next to the Cox family and was a member of the Salvation Army; she would brook no nonsense and was said to have chased children with a whip. Her husband worked for Johnson's coal merchants.

Harding Cook worked at the Mill; he kept ferrets (sometimes in his pockets) and did a lot of rabbiting. He let children fire his air rifle at lemonade tops balanced on a piece of metal. Fred Holtham also worked at the Mill; he called everyone Brother.

The Tanyards in Distons Lane. (A. Brain)

Distons Lane was once an old farm and although its name was changed to King Edward Street in 1902, it reverted back to its original name in 1908 by popular demand. As well as the tannery, the original gas works were at the east end of the lane near the churchyard. Houses, or rather cottages, were built on the east side by Mr Bliss c1870 in blocks of two and of four. The first were occupied by foremen and the latter by workers. The houses had tiny kitchens with black grates and box toilets; there was no heating and although the bedrooms had tiny fireplaces, the fire was only lit when someone was ill. Wash houses were shared and all the washing was done in coppers; a white stick was used to pound the washing and children were not allowed to touch this. Between the two large and four small houses were alleyways where there were hooks to hang washing lines on.

Mr Walt and Mrs Esther Keeley outside their cottage in Horsefair, now demolished and part of the tyre factory. (A. Brain)

This photograph was taken at the top of Bell Yard in the early 1900s. The children are actually standing in the Burford Road with Bell Yard leading to the left. The lady on the right is Polly Bateman.

Goddard's Lane between the Blue Boar and the Guildhall; this was known as the Bricks because the path was made of blue bricks. In the 1850s, Mr Goddard was landlord of the Crown and Cushion. This photograph was taken in the great frost and snow in February 1947; the gentleman is Joe Fowler. At the bottom of the lane is The Chequers public house. The bay window on the right was once the premises of the Horse and Groom.

G.H. Hannis on the London Road in the bad winter of 1947.